Craft or Christ

Uncovering witchcraft in the heart of the Christian Church

Michael S Fryer

Published by:

Father's House Congregation

Wales, UK

ISBN-13: 978-1543091670

For more information on the work of Michael Fryer, please visit:

www.FathersHouse.wales

Unless otherwise indicated, all Bible quotations are taken from the New International Version.

Contents

Foreword

The intention of ***Craft or Christ*** is to expose the extent to which the worldwide church has fallen into pagan practices, opening doors to witchcraft and false teaching. These practices are not just historical but are thriving in today's church.

The contents are meant to be provoking as well as informative and are the result of the way in which God has led me over the last seven years.

If you are seeking the truth according to scripture, you will not fail to be brought to some very radical choices, challenging the very foundations of Christian practices and traditions. It will prove to be very uncomfortable reading for many.

Craft or Christ also acts as a warning to those churches who embrace New Age practices and multi-faith teachings, as well as those who reject scripture through intellectualism and liberalism.

I encourage the reader to check out both the scriptural and historical basis for this warning. I believe that if it is not heeded, we will see devastating consequences for the coming generation and for our nations.

~ Mike Fryer

Introduction

In life we need clear guidelines to follow. We need to know what those guidelines are in order to teach and guide others. This is the responsibility of parenting, teaching, governing and enforcing within our society.

In 1973 I joined the Police Service, attending the Police Training Centre at Bridgend, South Wales. There I began my Police career by learning legal definitions by rote. I later attended the Detective Training Centre at Wakefield where, for three months I learned Criminal Law, again by rote. Although I found this method of learning very difficult, knowing Law in this way was essential when arresting offenders and dealing with them.

As I moved through the complicated and often drawn out legal process, which involved Solicitors, Barristers and the Courts, I was always aware of absolutes involved in each case.

One of the greatest dangers in bringing a case before the court, particularly the more complicated cases, is when confusion is introduced by the Defence in order to negotiate a lesser charge or to reduce the sentence. Only by knowing the case fully and having clear legal definitions planted solidly in one's mind can the investigating officers steer a proper course of action.

We need to know the defining precepts of our Christian faith which, over the last 2000 years has been infiltrated and influenced by paganism, witchcraft and idol worship, as it was during those times when the Nation of Israel entered into the practices of idolatry. Only such men as Josiah (2 Chronicles 34-36) and Hezekiah (2Kingsv18) were able to see clearly enough to stand against the flow of idolatry, remove all the idols and altars and to restore the temple following the guidance in the book of the Law.

Idolatry, New Age, witchcraft, political correctness and a desire to worship nature are acceptable practices in our society today. The general population is unaware that these practices are opposed to God. Such practices, which are even integrated into the Church have, over the centuries, confused our thinking about our Christian faith. In order to defuse the confusion and bring about a change, there is a need to follow the clear precepts of God's law and teach it correctly in these days. To do this we need to know both the precepts of God and also the tactics of Satan.

"My people are destroyed from lack of knowledge" - Hosea 4 v 6.

Some Churches in our Nation operate under such confusion. Confusion and ignorance surrounding the dates and practices of festivals is commonplace. Those festivals given by God in the book of Leviticus have been changed and adulterated so that we Christians align ourselves to pagan festivals instead of the festivals of God. Even over the question of Israel there is confusion. Our Saviour is clearly King of The Jews. He is returning to Israel, a land God has given to the Nation of Israel, yet many Churches are unable to see the clarity of scripture concerning these issues. We must remember that Satan is the master of confusion and it is he who tries to change the times and Laws that God Himself has set.

"He will speak against the Most High and oppress His saints and try to change the set times and the Laws" Daniel 7 v 25

The effect of not speaking out against such things is that our children have been and still are taught, as they were thousands of years ago, to worship other Gods. However, we seem oblivious to this and apathetic to all that is going on around us. In some cases there are Churches supportive of such idolatrous practices, as you will discover as you read on.

We have the Book, the Law, with its definitions of

who and how to worship, and the Holy Spirit to guide us through the confusion. But we need also to expand our knowledge about the pagan practices that are increasingly being followed in our Nation in order that we can identify them and speak out as Paul did in Acts 19, and inform the people that there is only one God! Like Paul, we need to feel greatly distressed at what we see.

This book is, therefore, an attempt to raise awareness of the truth of scripture and the precepts of God against the ritual practices of paganism, particularly in Wales. I have not written it to be an offence against any Christian leader or denomination! This is not an attack upon the persons but on the spiritual forces that are behind their actions which result in a false teaching of the Word of God, thereby affecting our children's understanding of scripture:

“You shall have no other gods before Me.”

You shall not make for yourself an idol in the form of anything in heaven above or on the earth beneath or in the waters below.

You shall not bow down to them or worship them; for I, the LORD your God, am a jealous God, punishing the children for the sin of the fathers to the third and fourth generation of those who hate Me” (Ex 20:3-5).

Roots and Origins of Paganism

Historians and pagans provide evidence today that until the end of the Eolithic age, around 12,000 BC, the grave was seen as a womb. Through this concept the craft known as witchcraft originated. Between that time and 7,000 years BC during the Palaeolithic age, the first representations of the "horned god" appear and the worship of such idols is practiced. Up to 3,000 years BC during the Neolithic age, we see the beginnings of the worship of moon goddesses and the horned god takes on solar characteristics. The Iron Age up to 1,000yrs BC continues with worship of the moon goddess and the horned god, also stone monuments are built.

Up to 100 BC, Greek and Egyptian pantheons develop, Isis predominates, obelisks are built, sunbursts are popularized and particular days are set aside for sun worship i.e. Sun Day. The Sphinx is built with all its references to the gods of the dead, which are also seen in the forms of the pyramids.

In the first century the strong pagan practices of Sun, Moon and earth worship infiltrate the newly formed Church with such symbols as sunbursts and halos.

This early Church then takes on the worship of "mother of God" and Icons and the practice of praying to the dead saints becomes the norm. Church architecture was influenced by causing church worshippers to face eastwards towards the rising sun.

Decoration in many Churches from 12th century onwards involved carvings in stone and wood of the "Green Man" depicting the god Cernunos. These carvings show the face of the god surrounded by leaves and often having leaves sprouting from the mouth and ears. These carvings can be seen all over the United Kingdom in such places of worship as Exeter Cathedral, around the crypt in Canterbury Cathedral and Holy Trinity Church in Coventry. You may find them in the architecture of your own Church, often high up or hidden behind roof trusses.

A photo of the Green Man taken from a document found on a pew in St. Peters Church, Pennal

Manchester Cathedral website advertises a

"Discovery Trail" directed at Key Stage 2 & 3 children to find the Green Man both inside and outside the building, followed by a workshop in which they design their own Green Man and create a clay plaque, based on their design. The website states "Images of him are to be found in over 1,000 mediaeval churches throughout Western Europe. In some churches, images of the Green Man outnumber images of Christ by 100 to 1"

I have heard arguments from clergy who state that the builders of these churches and cathedrals were not Christian and they carved these images without the knowledge of church leadership. However this cannot be accepted, as in the case of Pennal where the Green Man is seen in the stained glass window and in the case of Canterbury Cathedral where he is seen on the font.

The green man symbolizes forest demons, suffering souls, the trickster in the leaves and also depicts the god in pagan earth worship as well as the god of the dead. This god has also been called the green messiah. The green man can also be seen in architecture dating back 2000 years in India and throughout the Roman Empire.

During the Middle Ages pagan religions were virtually wiped out but secret pagan practices continued. In 1950 the practice of Wicca developed and has since gathered a large following. Witchcraft in general is now seeing a revival amongst those searching for a spiritual experience; just take a look at the number of websites answering children and teenagers' questions on the subject. For example, I bought a book on the Internet which teaches parents how to raise children in the Wiccan "faith"!

"Raising Witches" written by Ashleen O'Gaea, teaches how to bring up children using spells, incantations and pagan rituals. As a Governor of our local school, I was able to bring this to the school's Governing Body to raise awareness of the reality of this issue and to point out that it is against the will and word of God to be involved in such things.

When Jesus spoke to the Samaritan woman at the well, He made it unequivocally clear who we are to worship. It is our responsibility to make it clear to all, particularly those with responsibilities for children and to the children themselves that there is only one God.

If you were to take time to research children's literature as provided for their education in Celtic traditions, you may be surprised at the cohesive approach to teaching even young children of the festivals and traditions of paganism. I have already mentioned the Manchester Cathedral programme for school children in order to find the Green Man.

A lover Wales, tourist centres are “cashing in” on the history of their particular subject and making attractive, professional presentations, aimed at school pupils at junior level. Celtica in Machynlleth is one such example of this. This centre has produced, and sells to school visitors, a teaching aid which educates children about all the pagan seasons and festivals, the god Cernunos (and many others), sacrifices, beliefs and druid worship, all interspersed within the more practical information of tools, house-building and clothing, etc., in an engaging and attractive presentation. They also have an exhibition in which realistic-looking decapitated heads are hung from trees in order to tell the story of the sacrifices made by the Celts to the gods.

One purpose behind these activity centres is to attract, influence and engage our children in an understanding of paganism from an early age.

“Train a child in the way he should go and when he is old he will not turn from it” (Prov 22 v6).

The general concept of the historic and current pagan practice of witchcraft is that there are eight separate festivals all fulfilling a yearly cycle. These festivals are called Sabbats and are celebrated around the cycle of the seasons. The god and the goddess are central characters in these pagan myths.

The seasons trigger the birth and death of the god, which is that worshipped in connection with the sun. The god is both the son and the lover of the goddess.

The god is born by the goddess at “Yule” in December. The goddess returns to her maiden aspect in the Spring. The god and goddess grow up to be young adults, and at the vernal equinox the god falls in love with the goddess (his mother!) and they create a child. The god now lives inside the goddess.

At midsummer they are both at their peak of power and adulthood. The god's power begins to wane at Lammas and the goddess ages. The god hits old age and prepares to die at Samhain (Halloween) and the goddess grows with the god-child. After the god dies at Samhain and "returns to the womb of the goddess, he is reincarnated as his own child and is re-born at Yule.

~raft - Festivals and Sabbats

~nd February - CANDLEMAS:

Known as Imbolc, Oimelc and Lady Day. 'Candlemas' is the Christianized name for this sabbat.

'Imbolc' means, literally, 'in the belly' (of the mother). Pagans believe that this festival celebrates the time when the seed that was planted in her womb at the solstice is evolving as the new year grows.

'Oimelc' means 'milk of ewes', for it is also lambing season.

The holiday is also called 'Brigit's Day', in honour of the Irish goddess Brigit. At her shrine in the ancient Irish capital of Kildare, a group of priestesses (no men allowed) keep a perpetual flame burning in her honour. She was also considered a goddess of fire.

21st March - SPRING EQUINOX:

Known as Vernal Equinox Sabbat, it is the Festival of the trees and of Ostara and Rite of Eostre, and celebrated on the first day of spring.

This sabbat involves the worship of the goddess

Ostre (fertility goddess) from whom we get the name Easter.

The name 'Easter' was also taken from the name of a Teutonic lunar goddess, Eostre (from where we also get the name of the female hormone, oestrogen). Her chief symbols were the rabbit (Easter bunny) symbols of fertility, and the egg, the beginning of creation. In 325 AD the Church fathers joined in this celebration by moving away from the Levitical Feast of Passover during which Jesus was crucified as the Passover lamb. (See later references).

1st May - BELTANE:

Known as May Day, Round Day, Rudemas and Walpurgisnacht. This is celebrated on May Eve and May 1. May is the month which was named in honour of the goddess Maia, originally a Greek mountain nymph.

The original Celtic name for May Day is Beltane which comes from the Irish Gaelic 'Bealtaine' or the Scottish Gaelic 'Bealtuinn', meaning 'Bel-fire', the fire of the Celtic god of light (Bel, Beli or Belinus). He, in turn, is traced back to the Middle Eastern god Baal.

The Beltane celebration was, and still is, principally a time of lust, sexuality and fertility. It is of the hobby horse. The children's nursery rhyme, 'Ride a cock horse to Banbury Cross...' is a poetic demonstration of the festival. It then says '...to see a fine lady on a white horse' which is a reference to the annual ride of 'Lady Godiva' through Coventry. This festival is enacted in the May Day parades we see in our local towns and villages. The Puritans put an end to the custom of electing a May Queen which society has, for three hundred years, restored using a young girl, albeit no longer naked, to ride on the back of a lorry or tractor.

A pagan woman who appeared on the May Day Sunday BBC4 religious radio programme described how she and a large group of others had spent the night practicing this festival.

21st June - SUMMER SOLSTICE:

Known as Midsummer, Alban Hefin, and Litha, and celebrated on the first day of summer. Modern witches often refer to the festival by the name of Midsummer's Eve and this night is believed to be sacred. Customs surrounding it are many and varied. Some practitioners of witchcraft would stay up throughout the whole of this shortest night and keep watch in the centre of a circle of standing stones. They believe this would result in either their death or madness, or they would receive the power of inspiration to become a great poet or bard.

1st August - LAMMAS:

Known as Lughnasadh, August Eve, and the First Festival of Harvest.

Witches consider this date is a 'power point' of the Zodiac and is symbolized by the Lion, one of the 'tetramorph' figures found on the Tarot cards, the World and the Wheel of Fortune (the other three figures being the Bull, the Eagle, and the Spirit). Astrologers know these four figures as the symbols of the four 'fixed' signs of the Zodiac, and these naturally align with the four major Sabbats of Witchcraft.

21st September - MABON:

Held on Sept. 20-23, dependent on actual astronomical event. A lesser holiday, this is not widely celebrated except by the most pure Wiccan groups, especially those who are based in the works of Starhawk and other Dianic sects. This is the weavers festival and braiding of cords is done in the process of casting a spell to add to one's life—each person weaving for themselves what they wish and the coven as a whole weaving all the cords together to unite the power symbolically.

31st October- SAMHAIN:

Known as all Hallows Eve, All Saints Eve, Festival

of the Dead, and the Third Festival of the Harvest. Celebrated as a feast of the dead it is believed that the dead can return to the land of the living for this one night. Lanterns are used to help the dead find their way. Extra places are set at the evening dinner table and food is prepared for anyone who has died that year. At this festival the god Cernunos is worshipped. This is the same god as the green man but whereas the green man is worshipped in spring, Cernunos is worshipped in this autumn festival. You will read later on how this festival is practiced in a Welsh town.

21st December - WINTER SOLSTICE:

Known as Yule, Winter Rite, Midwinter, this festival is celebrated on the first day of Winter. It is associated with Nordic divination, Celtic fertility rites, and Roman Mithraism.

Martin Luther and John Calvin abhorred this festival and the Puritans refused to acknowledge it, much less celebrate it. The holiday is associated with the birth of older Pagan gods such as Oedipus, Theseus, Hercules, Perseus, Jason, Dionysus, Apollo, Mithra, and Horus. Many of them pre-dated Christianity.

It is the longest night of the year, the turning point when the days following grow longer as winter begins its passage into the coming spring. It is the time of goddess worship, the time when she gives birth to the divine Sun child who is both child and eventually lover and father of the next child in the cycle. Winter solstice for pagans is a time of feasting and the exchanging of gifts.

The evergreen tree, the holly and the ivy and the mistletoe were important plants of the season, all symbolizing fertility and everlasting life to the pagan. The Celtic Druids cut holly and mistletoe with a golden sickle on the sixth night of the moon in this month believing it to be an aphrodisiac, despite it being toxic. Aphrodisiacs were just part of the Yuletide menu in ancient times as reports indicate that the households were full of good food and drink.

The dating of Christmas has its origins in the Roman feast of the "Invincible Sun" which was celebrated on 25th December and this day honoured what the Romans believed was the birthday of this particular god.

My Elder pointed out a scripture to me which I am sure you will find interesting and applicable to this particular festival. To Israel God said:

"The laws of the nations are delusions, for it is the work of a craftsman's hands. He cuts down a tree in the forest with an axe; he adorns it with silver and gold" (Jeremiah 10 v 3&4).

The argument is, of course, that the early Christians transposed sacred festivals on to profane dates in order to "Christianize" them. This is not the explanation given by the early church fathers who said they wanted nothing at all to do with Jewish practices. In reality, as experience shows, paganism has flourished and Christianity has become weak and without influence in our society.

Personal Experience

My first encounters with such people were whilst I was a detective on the Drug Squad. I cultivated a number of informants, some of whom were practising witches. These informants, although they are drug users and dealers, would provide information about more serious offenders within the drug culture.

They would talk about their practices and the use of drugs such as LSD, Psilocybin, cannabis and amphetamines which are used to stimulate hallucinations as well as the speeding up of the physical functions of the body during such times.

All these drugs are necessary to the new indulgent form of paganism which had infiltrated and influenced the criminal community. Between the towns of Wrexham and Deeside (approx 20 miles apart), I learned that there were at least 25 covens practising in homes, woodlands and on mountain locations.

One of my male informants was a self-confessed practising witch who dealt in drugs. He would tell me of his trips to Leeds in order to buy witchcraft paraphernalia—apparently Leeds is a well-known centre for witchcraft, also of his trips to Glastonbury where witches would swap their latest methods and tactics for carrying out their practises.

He was fascinated by symbols such as upside-down crosses, ankhs, circles, pictures of demons, serpents and various gods. He was heavily tattooed with such symbols and his home was full of icons and statues.

I later arrested another of my informants, she being a practising witch who was addicted to amphetamine. When searching her home in the local estate I found her bedroom was painted black with a pentagram marked out on the floor.

Witchcraft paraphernalia was found in her room included coffin handles, plaques from churches, soil which she said was taken from fresh graves, upside-down crosses and various other symbols of Satanic worship.

She freely admitted that drugs were used by her to lure young people into her home for the purposes of satanic worship, which many times involved sexual acts.

I was regaled with many stories from a carpet fitter I knew who would regularly be required to replace carpets in homes where one or more rooms had been given over as witchcraft meeting places with, again, the pentagram and black-painted walls being the norm. My investigations at that time indicated that such activity was a growing national problem, but in my last seven years as a pastor, I have become convinced that various forms of witchcraft have become endemic within all strata of our society, aimed firstly at the children and at those desperately seeking a spiritual experience.

New Age

New "sanitised" forms of witchcraft and pagan practices are prevailing in our society today. The use of crystals in worship, the practice of divination, acupuncture and 'reiki' healing, levitation, hypnotism and mind control exercises such as psychic meditation, martial arts and yoga are accepted and are common place. Divination methods such as use of tarot cards and Ouija boards have also become very common, especially amongst children and young people.

In schools and colleges now Ouija boards are in common rooms alongside Monopoly and Scrabble.

A member of my congregation reported that her child's new R.E. teacher had attempted to teach the entire class how to meditate, using transcendental techniques. When challenged by the child, the teacher declared she was a "sort of Christian." The head teacher of the school was unaware of the dangers of this New Age activity, which is so subtle!

Any dabbling with psychic power can be extremely dangerous, opening up an innocent child to life-long problems and oppression, but the seriousness of these things seems to have bypassed the church in general. It appears that almost anything goes nowadays without question or challenge.

Many may remark why martial arts? During my Police service as a non-believer, I practised the art of “silent hands,” a form of martial art that used mind control to initiate attacks upon a victim. The use of discreet force to immobilise the victim is the aim.

My instructors, who were far more advanced than I could be, would spend hours gaining control over their heart beats and their minds in extreme temperatures by lying naked in snow for hours simply to have so much control on their bodies that they could both inflict and even receive extreme pain without effect. I have witnessed the devastating results of these eastern practices first-hand.

Why yoga you may ask? There are many forms of yoga but the ultimate purpose of all yoga is to bring the practitioner, whether they know it or not, into union with Brahman, a spirit God. The warm-up exercises alone are known as “Surya Namaskar”, also known as “Sun Salutation.”

They are, in fact, a series of positions created to worship the sun god called Baal. Traditionally these exercises are performed at dawn facing in the direction of the sun.

The practice of both yoga and martial arts will

result in the cooling off and drawing away of a believer from a vital relationship with Jesus.

Read on for spells associated with crystals in the practice of Wicca. We need also to understand that many of theology therapies such as reflexology, cytotoxology and iridology originate from pagan divination.

Twenty years ago whilst on CID, my colleagues and I arrested a man who had a Medical practice in a small Welsh village. He used the title Doctor and purported to be a Medical Practitioner whose expertise was in alternative medicine.

He advertised that, by using radiasthesia, he could determine what one's dietary needs should be. This impressive-sounding form of medical testing involved the patient paying a substantial fee to have a hair, including the root, taken from the head and tested.

Details of this test were not disclosed to the patient who would later return and be told of the result. This practice was extremely profitable to the doctor. In over 90% of cases, the doctor would tell them that their yeast intake was far too great.

We arrested this man on the grounds of complaints made by many female patients who claimed that he had indecently assaulted them. We soon discovered that he was not, in fact, a medical doctor but a long-distance lorry driver who had decided to change his name and practice in alternative therapies.

We soon had hundreds of complaints pouring in about the radiasthesia tests and found that he was in fact using a toggle on a piece of string to hang over the hair to give him his result. Radiasthesia, I came to understand, was simply divination. He was later convicted as a result of a six weeks trial at Crown Court.

In essence, New Age activities encourage us to either look inside ourselves for spiritual enlightenment, experience or growth and to find the potential to be god within each human being, or to seek a practical insight or remedy through means other than the revealed Word of God in the Bible.

This is in direct opposition to scripture! Instead of taking every thought captive to Christ and meditating on the Laws of God, people are invited to blank out their minds through meditation, which provides an open door for torment and oppression.

Today's Witchcraft

Today we hear much of Wicca and the practice of spells being made for good, and respect for the seasons, and for nature. Wicca follows the course of the god and goddess through the seasonal cycle, as I have previously explained, and is an avenue through which, by following the Sabbats, the individual can worship these gods.

This practice, known as the craft, has attempted to bring with it an air of respectability to make it acceptable in our society. The Wiccan is deceived by the idea that one can belong to a society with social, political and economic expectations that are brought about solely through loving the earth and the planet and the gods that they say dictate the yearly cycle of life.

The belief is that worship of the planet and the earth will bring about a peaceful and therefore prosperous society.

Wicca began in 1950, and the individual Wiccan follows the book of shadows, which is a journal of one's own life. The practice known as Wiccanning is often carried out in stone circles when blessings are prayed in such circumstances as bringing a child into their faith, or over a pregnant mother for the expected baby, or simply to invoke a certain power. The circle is key to this practice.

Stones are also important. For instance a prayer over a crystal is as follows.

"I empower this stone to attract all powers wondrous and good. May it empower (name of person) to take the next step in her journey".

A prayer involving an amethyst is as follows. "As this stone represents the child, let it draw positive energies, love, light, and health. As the wheel turns may her coming year be blessed with happiness and gifts from the lord and lady (god and goddess)."

You will probably have come across shops that sell such stones and crystals—this is the reason for such outlets. These stones are blessed by the Wiccan priests and priestesses, therefore having a spiritual influence upon the purchaser.

When the Wicca child grows older, ceremonies for the coming of age called Manning and Womanning are carried out within the stone circles. Each stage of development is followed giving glory to the god and goddess within the cycle or circle of life. When and wherever stone circles are found they can usually be associated with such practice.

According to Wicca, spells work by praying to the god and goddess and leaving it to them to decide how the spell should be carried out. Perhaps it is appropriate here to clarify the difference between Satanism and Wicca. Those involved in black magic, witchcraft or Satanism know the power of the enemy and, having chosen to serve Satan, use spells and incantations to send demons directly to afflict or oppress others in order to gain or obtain power and get their own way. Because of these differences, Wicca is often referred to as "White Magic".

I put it to you that at root there is no difference because the author of all magic arts is Satan, the enemy of God.

Today we see our bookshops, the Internet and the television screen full of Wicca teaching. There are many books teaching witchcraft practices such as

"Raising Witches" which teaches parents how to raise their children as Wiccan witches. The aim of Wicca is to influence our society through our children, through politics and the community.

I have led one Wiccan to the Lord and as a result have learned a great deal about these practices. However this person has now returned to the familiar ways and today continues to curse me. This person told me recently that a number of Wiccans were praying for my death on a weekly basis. They also fast and meet together regularly to pray against churches and Christian families.

Something Christians need to understand is that all witches really are opposed to God and to Christians. When I first began pioneering my Church I was told by a Wicca witch that I was being prayed for—I knew what was meant by that! We have also understood the consequences of such spiritual activity and have had to grow up in this area and begin to fight back according to the Word of God:

"The weapons we fight with are not the weapons of the world. On the contrary, they have divine power to demolish strongholds. We demolish arguments and every pretension that sets itself up against the knowledge of God, and we take captive every thought to make it obedient to Christ" (2 Cor 10:4-5).

Today witches throughout the world are doing more than praying, they are acting politically against the Christian message. In Australia this month, (April 2005) a witch who is in prison for sexual offences has complained to the Australian Victorian Civil and Administrative Tribunal (VCAT) about the Alpha course, which we know is a wonderful evangelistic tool.

Robin Fletcher, the self-described witch has asked

the VCAT to ban the course. There is a real possibility of this happening under the legislation of the VCAT, which came into force in Australia in 2001.

This type of legislation has already been brought before the UK Parliament and is likely to be re-introduced again soon. If this Serious Organised Crime and Police Bill is adopted, then this book would be illegal and I could be prosecuted for its publication.

I personally find it humorous that as a detective on the National Crime Squad, I was assigned to "Serious Organised Crime", targeting the top 200 criminals in the UK. But the fact is that I could soon find myself amongst that "elite" band, being arrested and charged by my former colleagues for doing no more than telling the truth about the number 1 criminal in the UK, Satan himself!

Machynlleth - the Return to Paganism

Paganism has been and still is a practice and culture that is now integrated into society and into the Church. This causes confusion amongst those who have no understanding of scripture, and also deceives those who have some knowledge but who are taught incorrectly. Machynlleth in Wales is an example of such a statement.

An artist's impression of the lantern effigy of the Horned God, Cernunos

Geographically Machynlleth is situated in central

Wales with a population of 2,500. It is an area which has a large number of stone circle sites built thousands of years ago, with some built more recently.

During the “Samhain” festival of 31st October 2004, press reports from the town showed that 2,500, mainly local people including many children, attended the festival.

Government grants had been given, together with the support of local businesses, to finance production of lanterns for the festival.

One huge lantern effigy, between 3-4m tall of the god Cernunos, (the green man) had been made by the local people. This god was the focus of the festival, which was used to beckon and invoke the dead. Children dressed up as Satan and witches and were photographed dancing before this god figure. Two of the most prominent local groups, Celtica and Elemental Earth were the organisers.

As they did last year, Celtica are again this year organising classes for the making of the god-figure and the lanterns. Elemental Earth has also been given a grant of £10,000 for the cost of the materials to do so. I have spoken to a member of Celtica who assured me that this is a religious event.

To add to the problems in the area, in a village

called Pennal situated four miles out of the town, the local Church in Wales' Vicar supports the festival. I found within his Church the Church diary which was distributed to the congregation last year. This gives details of the Samhain Festival and also advertises a production of 'Lord of the Flies'.

Standing stones found in the Vicar of Pennal's rear garden

This clergyman has written a book in which he describes his personal relationship with the green man, with an illustration of this horned god, describing the green man as a trusted companion.

In this book "Honest to Goddess", he talks of the divine feminine lady of wisdom, Sophia. The book contains references to Jesus and Jerusalem, which are written in lower case, with the names of the green man and Sophia beginning in capitals.

In the Church is a book of Zen, a Hindu god—Shiva, a Buddha and pictures of Sophia shown both in a white gown and bare-breasted.

I also found documents openly lying around concerning the green man and pictures of him as a horned god as well as copies of the Koran, the Talmud and the Bhagavad Gita.

The vicar has also opened up a chapel nearby called Capel Hagia Sophia, dedicated to the goddess Sophia. This is supported by the Bishop of Bangor who recently blessed the opening of this new chapel and, subsequently, wrote to me expressing full support for his vicar and all that he is doing.

There is a stone circle in the Churchyard (for which a grant was obtained) and there is also a stone circle in the garden at the Vicar's home, both are recent constructions.

One of the most worrying issues is that the vicar advertises for schools to visit his church and chapel.

This, coupled with the local organisations encouraging children to join the Samhain festival, is a recipe that can only bring death and not life to the future of this town but, because the Church is involved, the parishioners believe there is nothing wrong.

Sophia, as displayed on the wall at St Peter's church, Pennal

The Divine Feminine?

The recently built stone circle in the churchyard at St. Peter's Church, Pennal. This clearly shows the compass points

I have made enquiries, and I know of no other pagan festival in the United Kingdom that can compare even closely with the large number of attendees, the support, or the finance given to this pagan sabbat festival, held in Machynlleth.

I spoke to an American pastor recently who, like me, is shocked at the extent and openness of this situation.

An argument has been brought to me from the Bishop, who supports what is presented at Pennal regarding having symbols of other gods, such as Buddha and the Hindu god Shiva, which are in both the Capel Hagia and the Church at Pennal.

He states that this is a way of welcoming those of other faiths into the place of worship to Jesus to make them, as he says, “feel welcome.”

God makes it very clear in Exodus 20 v 23: “Do not make any gods to be alongside me”.

There is an important principle here: When Aaron made the calf the Israelites then chose to worship the calf idol as the god who brought them out of Egypt.

However God had directed that they should worship Him in the Tabernacle and the result was His refusal to abide with them.

We must remember at this point that it was Aaron, the high priest, who brought about the creation of the golden calf, which caused God to become so angry that He was about to destroy the Israelites until Moses spoke with Him.

It is apparent that Christian leaders, as well as those who are appointed as God’s adversaries, have successfully led us into idolatry in one way or another.

On the next page, you will see an image of the Hindu god Shiva, presented with a very familiar verse of Scripture from Matthew 19:14.

Directly behind the Shiva idol are the scripture words: "Suffer little children to come unto me and forbid them not……"

Take for example a former Christian worship leader from North Wales who trained for the ministry but has turned away from his faith and now embraces paganism, leading a small but growing group of pagans.

He argued in the local press that, whilst at theological college, he was unable to obtain satisfactory answers to his questions regarding pagan traditions within the church.

He asks, "What is the connection between the Christmas tree and Israel?" arguing that the symbolism of Christmas and Easter represent the pagan rather than the origins of Christian faith. Having rejected Jesus, he says druids and pagans are delighted that Christians worship in the same way as themselves. Symbols of the god Cernunos/green man can be found within his home.

It can only be when we as Christians turn away from any association with pagan practices and festivals that arguments such as this can be rejected by the church. Until then, his argument remains valid!

In the Bible, God has established specific times and feasts for his people in order that we remember all that He has done for us. We have changed these God-ordained times and Festivals and we now remember God, using pagan symbols as overt as the Golden Calf!

Images such as the egg and bunny representing fertility, the tree, holly and evergreens which represent everlasting life through the god and goddess, are not acceptable to the God of the Bible.

Deception, Subtlety & Infiltration of Witchcraft

Wicca is one of several traditions of witchcraft.

The name Wicca has its root in Anglo Saxon times: "wic", which means to bend or shape. This is exactly what is happening in our society. There is a bending of the word of God and the practice of true Christianity and it is being shaped into a form that is acceptable to all areas in society, including paganism and witchcraft. Very subtle but, in the eyes of witches, very successful as the Church gives credibility to such acts of Baal worship and society embraces it.

We see the figure of Buddha as demonstrating an acceptance of a multi-faith practice, giving respect to other faiths. However, in the practice of Wicca, altars that are built within the circle of this practice often have the figure of Buddha.

A more subtle approach to Wicca infiltration and the teaching of their festivals can be seen in the example of Caws Celtica, a company situated in Ceredigion, Wales which sells rounds of ewe's milk cheese using the names of witchcraft festivals i.e. "Lammas", being the August harvest festival and "Beltane", being the May festival. This company have just introduced new cheeses onto the market, namely "Samhain", a brie-style cheese and "Imbolc", a cheese containing Dill seed. I am sure these cheeses are very tasty, but my point is that our society is learning the names and ways of witchcraft through everyday living and if we, the Church, are unaware of these things, then we will be advertising these cheeses using their witchcraft names at the next Vicar's garden party! Remember how nursery rhymes have been used and are still used? And May Day parades as well? It is all very subtle.

Have you noticed the introduction of the abbreviations for the times we live in? Until recently BC was used regularly meaning Before Christ, and AD –Anno Domini, meaning Year of Our Lord. Now we see CE meaning Common Era and, of course, B.C.E. Wiccans are constantly trying to introduce such things without our noticing, in fact I found out about this new dating system through my theological college lecturer who used it.

As I have already stated, Church architecture and decoration include many examples of the presence of the god Cernunos, depicted as the green man and many of us worship Jesus as this devil

Circles are very important in the practice of witchcraft, being used for spell making and ritual, and are often referred to as Quarters. These represent in Wicca practice the direction points of the compass, the quarter invoking and inviting directional qualities. A practicing Wicca told me recently how she practices in this way. She stands in a circle and, using the points of the compass, she places symbols of the earth, fire, water and air onto it and dedicates all things in the geographical area back to the god and goddess and the earth. This she does weekly.

We find historically built stone circles ranging throughout the land, ancient circles such as Stonehenge and the one at Cerrig Arthur near Barmouth, about 12 miles outside Machynlleth. The map book reports that there is also a possible ancient stone circle at "Eglwys Gwyddelod" in Pennal, near Machynleth. Often druid practices involve the making of stone circles and we can find druidic circles formed in more recent years in towns and villages all over Wales. The most recent stone circle of which I am aware is that found in St Peter's Churchyard, Pennal, built only in the last few years.

This year we had a family holiday in Cyprus. We stayed near Paphos, the centre of Aphrodite's worship where tourism is tied directly to this goddess, and such places as Aphrodite's pool, where she is supposed to have washed, are central tourist attractions.

This is a nation that is known for its Christian heritage, resulting from Paul's visit when he took the Gospel to the Island in the first century, but goddess worship has been subtly introduced to the Church there, giving an opening to paganism which is now being used as the focal point of their heritage.

We visited a Greek Orthodox church in Helios Bay which was full of icons. Whilst there, my eight-year-old daughter began to have pain in her ears and we realised that she was clearly having an adverse spiritual reaction to something in the Church.

When we looked up on the ceilings we saw paintings of angels with snake-like symbols coming out of their ears. There were two paintings of the skull and crossbones, an ugly gargoyle figure over the sanctuary and a number of paintings of a woman holding what appeared to be a child. Many would say that this was Mary with baby Jesus and move on, however my daughter asked why the baby looked like a man. He did!

The face of the baby was depicted as an adult and the reason is as follows: Osiris is a common figure in Egyptian burial practice; he is considered to be the lord of the afterlife and can be seen in a great deal of artwork on ancient Egyptian coffins signifying that the dead are under the power of

Osiris. In Egyptian paganism it is believed that Isis is both the sister and the wife of Osiris and also the mother of the god Horus.

Horus is often shown either as a Pharaoh or a miniature adult. Often these pictures of the woman and child, as seen in Catholic Churches, have the sun depicted behind their heads, called a “sunburst.” All sunburst symbols in Egyptian, pagan and Catholic worship have their origins in sun worship.

In the Pennal church, there is a painting of a goddess holding a child whose face is set in front of the pagan symbol of the Celtic cross, the circle of quarters of witchcraft, which represents, as I have already stated, four seasons of worship of the god and goddess, not the crucifixion. The woman in this painting is dressed in fineries and gowns of position and power and she is holding the lilies of death. The Church is depicted to her lower right thus represented as being subservient to her as is the man-child, the god Horus.

The worship of the gods of Osiris, Horus and Isis are evidenced in the study of the sphynx and the pyramids which contain writings about these gods dating back to 660BC. In 2000 years from now, if the Lord hasn’t returned, historians will say the same thing about many churches, that the people of this present century worshipped these gods.

Photograph of painting from Pennal Church of the goddess with man-child

Catholic Sunburst

Celtic Cross with 'triquetra', used in Catholic church as a representation of the Holy Trinity, but an ancient symbol of the threefold nature of a Celtic goddess or the three elements of earth, air and water, more recently adopted by Wicca.

A Cross in a circle with a circle at its centre is a witchcraft symbol. I had a Christian friend who once sent me a book on Celtic Christianity. The cover had this type of cross. The Celtic cross as already stated is actually a witchcraft symbol showing the four quarters of the seasonal aspects of the sun.

The Celts divided the year into eight, demonstrating in this symbol four cross quarter days: Samhain, Imbolc Beltane and Lammas, and the times of the remaining four witchcraft festivals. This cross is not in any way connected with the Cross of Christ.

I have read and heard the argument that all these symbols, along with the changes of Sabbath worship and the movements of the feasts were all ways through which the Church witnessed to the pagans to bring them to the worship of Jesus.

Historically this is unfounded as the apostles Peter and Paul maintained Sabbath worship as, of course, Jesus did. Neither Jesus nor any of the apostles accommodated anything which opposed the direct Word of God. They kept the Feasts of the Lord as He had commanded, at fixed times, according to the Word in Leviticus 23 v 2. They never attempted or suggested a change to times and laws as a way to witness truth. They would never have used pagan symbols to witness Christ to the pagans of the day.

In fact, Paul spoke out against the Galatian church which was composed of gentile believers, converted from the worship of other gods. These people had practised pagan festivals on the appointed days and seasons as I have described but, on conversion, in opposition to scriptural ordinances, they began to turn back to their old ways.

In Galatians 4 v 8-11, Paul makes this very directive statement which admonishes them for this:

"Formerly, when you did not know God, you were slaves to those who by nature are not gods. But now that you know God-- or rather are known by God--

how is it that you are turning back to those weak and miserable principles? Do you wish to be enslaved by them all over again? You are observing special days and months and seasons and years! I fear for you, that somehow I have wasted my efforts on you."

Paul then teaches in Colossians 2 v 16 & 17 that we cannot be judged by what we eat, drink or by days and festivals etc. He was teaching a pagan community who believed that Saturday was an unlucky day because it was the day of Saturn and was involved in other superstitious practices to bring them salvation. Paul was saying to them that Salvation is through Jesus and Him alone.

Within a few short years after Paul's death, the newly-formed church in Rome, and consequently, churches throughout the world, had turned back to the weak and miserable principles that Paul talked about. Did he really waste his time?

We must remember that it was the Romans who destroyed the Temple in 70AD and murdered an estimated 6000,000 Jews during that time. It was Hadrian in AD 69-79 who outlawed the practice of the Jewish Religion and particularly the observance of the Sabbath. Historic evidence shows that changes were made to appease Roman Emperors who, in the first and second centuries, were sun worshippers. This, coupled with the statements made by the early Bishops not to align themselves with the Jews and their worship, gives us strong evidence that the arguments as stated are futile.

But whatever view you take, the outworking is that, rather than the changes influencing the pagan community and leading the people completely away from the worship of other gods, as commanded in the Ten Commandments, the opposite has taken place. Pagans have infiltrated many churches and influenced Christians throughout the centuries to unwittingly follow pagan practice.

We also see today how Freemasonry, which is a pagan practice, is infiltrating the church and deceiving Christians. Within twenty miles from my home there are Churches who advertise that the Freemasons are leading Carol services. One advertises that they lead the Mother's Day service and another that they will be running certain Sunday services.

The leaders of these Churches cannot deny they know the spiritual opposites involved and yet they pursue this relationship. For Freemasons the credibility of involvement with a Christian Church, combined with the marketing of good works and fundraising such as the giving of the proceeds of Carol services to the poor, as was the case in

Wrexham Parish Church during the Christmas 2004, deceives those who sincerely want to worship the one and true God.

We need to take time to look deeper into these deceptive subtleties which are well-established and are influencing every aspect of our society.

I recently obtained a comprehensive list of leading freemasons in each county throughout England and Wales and, unsurprisingly, it revealed that many ordained clergy are occupying positions of high authority within the organisation. These men are without doubt opposing God through this practice.

During my 27yrs in the Police service I met and worked with many who were involved at many levels in Freemasonry. Many of these men were good-hearted people who claimed to be Christian in some form or other and for whom, as colleagues, I had great respect.

I was a member of a murder investigation team involving a Police Sergeant who had violently murdered his lovely wife and mother of two children. This sergeant and his two colleagues of the same rank, all three of whom were in charge of the Police area where he worked, were Freemasons in the same Lodge, and I recognised among them an unhealthy social life that made me ask serious questions about Freemasonry as I came to see how it was rooted in the opposite spirit.

I found that friends and colleagues who were Freemasons, with whom I had enjoyed a good relationship before I became a Christian, began to find me difficult. Relationships began to break down and, likewise, I found them just as difficult to work with.

All this is not surprising when you realise that Freemasonry openly embraces every faith and religion and is firmly rooted in the worship of Isis, the sun god. Going back some five thousand years to the secret societies of ancient Egypt, Masons can see all the signs, symbols and postures they adopt displayed on the walls of Egyptian tombs

The "all-seeing eye of God"--a symbol of Freemasonry that originates from ancient Egyptian worship of Osiris

The initiation ceremony into the lodge involves the new recruit being prepared as a condemned heretic on his way to the gallows. However, in the third degree ceremony, he is initiated by lying back into a coffin or onto a black sheet with his head hooded to be helped up again by the hand of a fellow Mason into the new resurrection into Freemasonry. As he progresses through the order he is given a secret name for God: Jah-bul-on. 'Jah' standing for Jehovah, 'bul' for Ba'al and 'On' for the Egyptian god, On. This is definitely not the Christian God of Abraham, Isaac and Jacob!

It is not surprising that being born into new life with Jesus would, in the spirit realm, offend these who are born again into the worship of Baal, the word Baal meaning Lord, Master or Owner. The name of Jesus Christ, our Saviour, Master, Lord and God is simply not allowed in a masonic lodge.

The deception occurs because those entering into the early degrees of the order have no understanding of the oaths they take and these are not revealed until much farther up the scale. At the thirteenth degree in the Scottish Rite, Royal Arch, the candidate musts wear to keep the secrets of a fellow mason, "murder and treason not excepted" and masons are obligated under blood oaths to assist and help a fellow mason in trouble whether legal or illegal.

At the twenty-fifth degree, oaths are taken

specifically regarding worship of Osiris, whilst the 33rd degree reveals Lucifer worshipped as God!

In some police operations briefings would take place involving over one hundred detectives at a time, particularly on the National Crime Squad, the unit I retired from, when investigators would come together from all over the UK.

I would walk into the briefing room, often a large gymnasium or hall, and after a short time would be able to sense tensions and difficulties with officers I had never met before, or with those I had known but not seen since my conversion, but all of whom I found out were Freemasons-- such was the spiritual dimension of light and darkness. Christians need to wake up and realise that Freemasonry is the opposite spirit to Christianity.

Today, this once secretive body of people are now revealing themselves and suggesting that they are a Christian organisation doing good works, having even recently registered themselves as a religion! Yes they do give to Charity but the one whom they worship is not the one who can bless, no matter how much money they give.

There is much more to say on this subject and there are many excellent books for the Christian who wants to break free from involvement in Freemasonry; I could write for a long time but my purpose is to provide an overview of the work of Satan in the church and to highlight the traps and deceptions against the Word of God to provoke and encourage revelation and understanding in the reader.

Ron G Campbell, who has written extensively on this subject, quotes from one of the many Freemasonry resources:

"The veneration which Masons have for the East confirms the theory that it is from the East that the Masonic cult proceeded, and that this bears a relation to the primitive religion whose first degeneration was sun worship"

~ Bazot, "Masonry Defined"

"He said to me, 'Do you see this, son of man? You will see things that are even more detestable than this.' He then brought me into the inner court of the house of the LORD, and there at the entrance to the temple, between the portico and the altar, were about twenty-five men. With their backs toward the temple of the LORD and their faces toward the east, they were bowing down to the sun in the east (Ezekiel 8:15-16)."

The Definitions of Scripture

In my introduction I mentioned the need to know legal definitions. So what does the Bible tell us about the festivals we are to keep and how does God define them? Paul teaches us that our faith is rooted in that of the Jews, through Christ Jesus, a practising Jew in Romans 11 v 17-18—the root supports us.

Paul describes Jesus as the Head of The Church and as a servant of the Jews in Romans 15 v 8.

To refer to all the Festivals of The Lord we can look at the book of Leviticus Chapter 23. If you recall I mentioned earlier that Satan tries to change the times--times are very significant!

In 2 Chronicles 12:32 David enrols the help of the tribe of Issachar because they knew the times they were in.

In Esther 1: 10-13 Xerxes consulted the wise men because they understood the times.

God gives us fixed times or designated times to worship. About the timing of the festivals He says "These are My fixed times, the fixed times of the Lord". Why is that?

At the time the feasts were given the Egyptians

were worshipping the sun god and goddesses and they had specific times to do so. Remember the Israelites had just left the Egyptian community and would have been involved in the calendar pattern of such worship.

For instance, during the month of August the Egyptians worshipped Horus and Osiris at the temple of Ra. The beginning of the feast of Osiris was at the beginning of September. In October, the feast of Wasir (Osiris) in Abydos.

In January the day of the keeping of the things of Osiris, and the festival of jubilation of Osiris. In February the feast of Osiris, and on it goes.

Osiris - judge of the dead

Rä - the Sun God

The Canaanites were also worshipping idols in this fashion and therefore the Lord, who called Israel to be a holy people (the word 'holy', meaning to be separated).

He called Israel to be separated from all connections with pagan worship, even to giving them the dates which, as stated, He fixed in order to keep the Nation separated. Sadly we have not remained separate because we have returned to the dates of the pagans.

However, these are the Festivals the Lord gave us in Chapter 23 of Leviticus:

The LORD said to Moses, "Speak to the Israelites

and say to them: 'these are my fixed times, the fixed times of The LORD, which you are to proclaim as sacred occasions."

(This particular translation is from the Jewish Study Bible, all other translations are from NIV which speaks of appointed times, some translations speak of designated times).

The Sabbath

"'There are six days when you may work, but the seventh day is a Sabbath of rest, a day of sacred assembly. You are not to do any work; wherever you live, it is a Sabbath to the LORD."

The Passover and Unleavened Bread

"'These are the Lord's appointed feasts, the sacred assemblies you are to proclaim at their appointed times: The Lord's Passover begins at twilight on the fourteenth day of the first month.

On the fifteenth day of that month the Lord's Feast of Unleavened Bread begins; for seven days you must eat bread made without yeast. On the first day hold a sacred assembly and do no regular work.

For seven days present an offering made to the LORD by fire. And on the seventh day hold a sacred assembly and do no regular work.'"

Firstfruits

The LORD said to Moses, "Speak to the Israelites and say to them: 'When you enter the land I am going to give you and you reap its harvest, bring to the priest a sheaf of the first grain you harvest.

He is to wave the sheaf before the LORD so it will be accepted on your behalf; the priest is to wave it on the day after the Sabbath. On the day you wave the sheaf, you must sacrifice as a burnt offering to the LORD a lamb a year old without defect, together with its grain offering of two-tenths of an ephah of fine flour mixed with oil--an offering made to the LORD by fire, a pleasing aroma-- and its drink offering of a quarter of a hin of wine. You must not eat any bread, or roasted or new grain, until the very day you bring this offering to your God. This is to be a lasting ordinance for the generations to come, wherever you live."

Feast of Weeks

"'From the day after the Sabbath, the day you brought the sheaf of the wave offering, count off seven full weeks. Count off fifty days up to the day after the seventh Sabbath, and then present an offering of new grain to the LORD. From wherever you live, bring two loaves made of two-tenths of an ephah of fine flour, baked with yeast, as a wave offering of firstfruits to the LORD.

Present with this bread seven male lambs, each a year old and without defect, one young bull and two rams. They will be a burnt offering to the LORD, together with their grain offerings and drink offerings--an offering made by fire, an aroma pleasing to the LORD.

Then sacrifice one male goat for a sin offering and two lambs, each a year old, for a fellowship offering. The priest is to wave the two lambs before the LORD as a wave offering, together with the bread of the firstfruits. They are a sacred offering to the LORD for the priest.

On that same day you are to proclaim a sacred assembly and do no regular work. This is to be a lasting ordinance for the generations to come, wherever you live. "'When you reap the harvest of your land, do not reap to the very edges of your field or gather the gleanings of your harvest. Leave them for the poor and the alien. I am the LORD your God.'"

Feast of Trumpets

The LORD said to Moses, "Say to the Israelites: 'On the first day of the seventh month you are to have a day of rest, a sacred assembly commemorated with trumpet blasts. Do no regular work, but present an offering made to the LORD by fire.'"

Day of Atonement

The LORD said to Moses, "The tenth day of this seventh month is the Day of Atonement. Hold a sacred assembly and deny yourselves, and present an offering made to the LORD by fire. Do no work on that day, because it is the Day of Atonement, when atonement is made for you before the LORD your God. Anyone who does not deny himself on that day must be cut off from his people. I will destroy from among his people anyone who does any work on that day. You shall do no work at all. This is to be a lasting ordinance for the generations to come, wherever you live. It is a sabbath of rest for you, and you must deny yourselves. From the evening of the ninth day of the month until the following evening you are to observe your sabbath."

Feast of Tabernacles

The LORD said to Moses, "Say to the Israelites: 'On the fifteenth day of the seventh month the Lord's Feast of Tabernacles begins, and it lasts for seven days. The first day is a sacred assembly; do no regular work. For seven days present offerings made to the LORD by fire, and on the eighth day hold a sacred assembly and present an offering made to the LORD by fire. It is the closing assembly; do no regular work.

"'These are the Lord's appointed feasts, which you

are to proclaim as sacred assemblies for bringing offerings made to the LORD by fire--the burnt offerings and grain offerings, sacrifices and drink offerings required for each day. These offerings are in addition to those for the Lord's sabbaths and in addition to your gifts and whatever you have vowed and all the freewill offerings you give to the LORD."

"'So beginning with the fifteenth day of the seventh month, after you have gathered the crops of the land, celebrate the festival to the LORD for seven days; the first day is a day of rest, and the eighth day also is a day of rest.

On the first day you are to take choice fruit from the trees, and palm fronds, leafy branches and poplars, and rejoice before the LORD your God for seven days. Celebrate this as a festival to the LORD for seven days each year. This is to be a lasting ordinance for the generations to come; celebrate it in the seventh month. Live in booths for seven days: All native-born Israelites are to live in booths so your descendants will know that I had the Israelites live in booths when I brought them out of Egypt. I am the LORD your God.'"

So Moses announced to the Israelites the appointed feasts of God.

The meanings of these Feasts to Christians are made

so clear in all that Jesus did. Jesus is the fulfilment of the feasts as He stated He was in Matthew 5. These meanings are as follows in a simplified form as the full teaching on these festivals would require a book in itself, but I am sure you will enjoy studying them yourself.

Passover - 14th of Nissan - The significance in Christ is the crucifixion, the Lamb of God being slain to free us from the slavery of Sin. For us it is the new birth through repentance and acceptance of Jesus.

Unleavened Bread - 15-21st Nissan, represents the burial of Christ and our repenting of Sin, removing the leaven which is sin from our lives and putting off the old ways.

First Fruits (Pentecost) begins on 18th of Nissan – speaks of Jesus' Resurrection and is to us the putting on of the new ways through discipleship in Jesus. Pentecost begins after 49 days have elapsed after First fruits, it is the time of the giving of the Law at Sinai and is seen in Jesus as exaltation. For us this means Baptism in the Spirit. Two loaves are waved at this feast representing for us one loaf for the Jews and one for the Gentiles bringing them together under the banner of Jesus, meaning the beginning of the Church.

Tabernacles begin with the Feast of Trumpets on

1st Tishri which signifies defeating the enemy and for us the placing of the Armour of God over us. The trumpet, meaning Judgment will be when Jesus returns to judge the world.

Day of Atonement is on 10th Tishri which is the time that the Priest entered The Temple and atoned for the sins of Israel. For us we recognized that Jesus atoned for our sins.

Tabernacles is the feast remembering that God dwelt with the Israelites in the Desert. For us this speaks of Jesus, born to dwell amongst men and His future coming-again to dwell in Jerusalem as King of The Jews.

The Jews have not stopped celebrating the Feasts of The Lord. We see that Ezekiel speaks of the Millennial era and clearly shows the continuance of the celebration of Passover – Ezekiel 45; 21-24, Unleavened Bread; also 45:21-24, Tabernacles 45; 25 and also New year 45; 18-20.

We also see Tabernacles in Zechariah 14; 16-18, which says this:

"Then the survivors from all the nations that have attacked Jerusalem will go up year after year to worship the King, the Lord Almighty, and to celebrate the Feast of Tabernacles. If any of the peoples of the earth do not go up to Jerusalem to worship the King, the Lord Almighty, they will have no rain."

I have said that the Lord gave us fixed times and has provided us with exact dates for each of these Feasts, which are set in the Jewish calendar. For example, Passover is on 14th of the month of Nissan in accordance with scripture. In the Christian calendar for this year (2005) this falls on 23rd of April. Jesus fulfils all these feasts and He can be seen in every detail.

We see also in Scripture that He attended and celebrated them. For example:

He went to the Synagogue on the Sabbath - Luke 4 v 16

When it was time for Passover Jesus went up to Jerusalem to the temple - John 2 v 13

Whilst He was in Jerusalem at the Passover feast - John 2 v 23

The Passover Feast was near - John 6 v 4

Jesus is at the Feast of Tabernacles - John 7v 14

At the Feast of Tabernacles (called the Greatest Day) Jesus said, "If anyone is thirsty, let him come to me and drink - John 7 v 37

Jesus at the Feast of Dedication - John 10 v 22

Jesus calls at Bethany on His way up to Jerusalem for Passover - John 11 v55 & 12v1

The Last Supper—Jesus Celebrates Passover and eats the Passover meal as well as following with the ceremonial washing - John 13

The Disciples Celebrate the Feasts:

All together at the Feast of Weeks - Pentecost - Acts 2.

Paul keeps the Sabbath - Acts 17 v 2, Acts 18 v 4

Paul keeps Pentecost - Acts 20 v 6.

You will probably ask the question, “Wasn’t Jesus arrested, crucified and didn’t He rise from the dead during this time of Passover, and don’t we celebrate this time of our Lord at Easter, which this year was in March?” The answer is yes, but the early Christians didn’t. They continued to celebrate the feast of Passover, remembering the significance of the Cross!

Although we can trace the controversy of Easter and Passover back to Bishop Sixtus in 116 AD, it was actually between 189 and 199 that Bishop Victor of Rome supported a move away from remembering the crucifixion at Passover to Easter Sunday worship and threatened to excommunicate anyone who didn't follow his direction.

However, it wasn't until 325 AD, after much pressure from Gentile Bishops that the Council of Nicea declared the following:

"It seems to everyone a most unworthy thing that we should follow the custom of the Jews in the celebration of this most Holy solemnity, who, polluted wretches, having stained their hands with nefarious crime, are justly blinded in their minds. It is fit, therefore, that, rejecting the practice of this people, we should perpetuate to all future ages the celebration of this rite, in a more legitimate order… We desire to have nothing in common with this so hated people, (referring to the Jews and their practices and feasts) for the Redeemer has marked out another path for us."

The Council of Nicea then changed the date of the celebration of the Crucifixion and Risen Lord to a date in the Calendar which fell in line with pagan worship, thereby replacing Passover and completely ignoring the date given by God in Leviticus.

The British Calendar Act of 1751 refers to this in part 111, stating the following:

"And whereas according to the rule prefixed to the book of Common Prayer of the Church of England,

Easter day is always the first Sunday after the first full moon which happens next after the one and twentieth day of March, and if the full moon happens upon a Sunday, Easter day is the Sunday after; which rule was made in conformity to the decree of the said General Council of Nicea, for the celebration of the said Easter."

When examining the early church in Wales, we see that the Festivals of the Lord were followed in so much as Passover was seen as the time of the crucifixion and the Sabbath was kept on its correct day being the seventh day of the week. However, Augustine came to the land with the authority of Rome and forced the Christians in Wales to change their worship to be in line with the Decree of Nicea, so the Welsh Church reluctantly moved from the Festivals of the Lord and the Sabbath to those that are held by the Church today. What we misunderstand about Augustine is that he was anti-Semitic, as was the Roman Church at that time.

This is some of what Augustine said about the Jews:

"The Jews hold Him, the Jews insult Him, the Jews bind Him, crown Him with thorns, dishonour Him with spitting, scourge Him, overwhelm Him with reviling, hang Him upon the tree, pierce Him with a spear, the Jews killed Him."

(He makes no mention of the part played by the

Gentiles in the punishment and death of Our Lord.)

In another sermon, Augustine says, "The Jews are wilfully blind to Holy Scripture, lacking in understanding and haters of the truth." (It was the Jews who, to this day, follow scripture and it was Augustine who moved away from Scripture concerning the Festivals and their dates because of his hatred of the Jews).

What happened was that, with a desire to have nothing to do with the Jews and with a desire to appease the pagan world, the Church set the date for the celebration of the Sacrifice of the Passover lamb - Jesus of Nazareth, which should have been in accordance with scripture on 14th of Nissan to a date that followed the pagan sabbat of the Spring Equinox and the worship of Ostre the goddess of fertility. We have a similar situation with Christmas and the change from the Sabbath to Sunday – Sunday worship, a day on which the Romans worshipped the Sun, the pagan Festival on 21st December being the winter solstice celebration of the birth of the sun god.

As most Theologians would agree, Jesus, was almost certainly born during the Feast of Tabernacles, the Festival when God tells the Israelites to celebrate the time when He 'tabernacled' with them in the desert.

Jesus fulfilled this by coming down from heaven to tabernacle with His people, and He will do so again as we have seen in the book of Zechariah, the Millennial period.

No wonder society today is confused. The Church has failed to give proper direction and has allowed confusion to enter into social practices today.

1 Corinthians 10 v 21 says: “You cannot drink the cup of the Lord and the cup of demons too; you cannot have a part in both the Lord’s table and the table of demons”

In the Church today we have feet in both camps, worshipping Jesus through pagan ritual and during pagan festivals which bear no resemblance to the Festivals the Lord gave us.

How many of us can really say that we are truly salt and light, as Jesus called us to be?

Feasts and Festivals of "The Church"

In general, the denominational church keeps what is known as Principal Holidays and Festivals and Greater Holidays.

According to the Book of Common Worship and the Alternative Service book, the Principal days are Easter day, Christmas day, Maundy Thursday, Good Friday and every Sunday in the year.

None of these holidays have their times rooted in scripture, but they are rooted in paganism, so much so that for this year, 2005 as an example, because of the spring equinox, the festival of the goddess Ostre, Easter was on 27th March.

The Church calendars tell us that Pentecost is 49 days after this time which, this year, puts Pentecost on 15th May and not 13th June as it should be.

Because the main dates are all incorrect then all the other festivals are thrown and have become tainted by pagan practice. For instance, God's dating for Pentecost, which is actually the Feast of Weeks, should fall 49 days plus 1 day after Passover which would place it on 22nd May this year, separating it totally from any pagan worship. Pentecost, God tells us, is a celebration of the giving of the law of

God which says that we should not worship other idols, and is an important time.

The Festivals in the Church calendars go from the naming of Jesus on 1st of January to the conversion of Paul through to many days to celebrate biblical figures such as the apostles and angels. Are we to worship these and remember them above the festivals of God?

Lesser Festivals and commemorations are in memory of people like Hilary, Bishop of Poitiers celebrated on 13th January, to Ann, the mother of Mary on 26th July and William law, Mystic, non juror b.1761.

I don't know where the idea came from for all of this but it has resulted in the Church having saints' days when the congregation are led into prayer for the dead. I have been unable to find any clear scriptural base for any of these Holidays and festivals.

I know there will be those who will say that a new calendar started on the birth of Christ, but the apostles didn't think so! There may be those who say that I am reading into Old Testament law but Jesus didn't say that He was creating new festivals or laws.

In fact He said "Do not think that I have come to

abolish the Law or the Prophets; I have not come to abolish them but to fulfil them. I tell you the truth, until heaven and earth disappear, not the smallest letter, not the least stroke of a pen will by any means disappear from the Law until everything is accomplished. Anyone who breaks one of the least of these commandments and teaches others to do the same will be called least in the Kingdom of Heaven." - Mathew 5 v 17-19.

I wish to make it very clear here that I am NOT advocating adopting Jewish Rabbinical Law as defined in the Mishnah or the Talmud or the specific laws given to the Jewish people by God.

As Gentile believers we need to understand, as Paul taught the Galatians, that we are not bound by the ceremonial laws such as ritual purity and specific foods.

Acts 21 makes it very clear that Paul, as a Jew, followed such laws, but the Gentile believer is bound only by the commands given to Moses on Mount Sinai, which God wrote with his own finger.

What I am advocating is that we do not follow pagan worship!

Exodus 23 v33 says:

"Do not let them (the Canaanites, etc) live in your

land, or they will cause you to sin against me, because the worship of their gods will certainly be a snare to you"

One such snare that the church has fallen into is Replacement Theology, a subject on which I teach at length within the Hidden Treasure course which I have written and taught throughout the UK.

This theology was founded by the early church fathers Eusebius, Luther, Augustine, Jerome and others who spoke against the Jewish people and their traditions, on occasion calling them swine and demons.

As a result the early church pulled away from association with all things Jewish and from the Jewish festivals and began the teaching that the church had now replaced Israel. The early church then led the persecution of the Jewish Nation and from that time on the false teaching that the church is the spiritual Israel became embedded in our theology, despite Paul's clear teaching in the book of Romans to the contrary.

Examples of Replacement theology can be seen in such as Matthew Henry's commentaries. In his concise commentary of Luke 17v20-37, he states "when Christ came to destroy the Jewish nation by the Roman armies" and in Luke 21v25-28 he states" when Christ came to destroy the Jews, he came to redeem the Christians who were persecuted and oppressed by them."

In scripture, we see this theology described by the Lord when he speaks to John in Revelation 2v9 and 3v9 as follows: "I know the slander of those who say they are Jews and are not but are a synagogue of Satan."

Who can these people be? They can only be those that say the church replaces Israel and are, therefore, as the Lord has described here.

However, when we examine some commentaries, particularly study notes often included within bible translations, we see, as I have found in the Life Application NIV Bible, comments which bend and twist the scripture into a slander.

For example, it contains this comment: "The synagogue of Satan means that these Jews were serving Satan's purposes and not God's when they gathered to worship"

As previously mentioned, the word wicca/witchcraft means to bend or to shape. Such notes clearly bend and re-shape the truth and can only be rooted in the witchcraft spirit, which is one of deception that has successfully deceived Christians throughout the centuries.

Had we remained true to the Word of God and had not subjugated the Jews, we would not have fallen so deeply into such deception. When we have separated ourselves from pagan worship and false theology, I sincerely believe we will witness the power of God coming back and visiting His true church once more.

Spiritual Consequences for the Land

What are the consequences of sin in our nation?

We see in Genesis that when Adam and Eve walked in the garden they wanted for nothing, the land produced all they needed. After the fall man had to work the land in order to produce and it becomes cursed.

When all is being restored back to God, and as we enter the period of the redemption of Israel, God says in Isaiah 27 v 6 that He will make the land of Israel blossom and bud and fill the world with fruit. In Isaiah 35v1-2 God says that the land will be glad and the wilderness will rejoice. The land then is clearly blessed.

From the Bible we see there are clear consequences to sin that not only affect ourselves but the land in which we live.

These consequences are seen through the Spiritual principles that we see in scripture that land is sensitive to the sinful behaviour of its inhabitants. Leviticus 18 describes the sexual sins we must not fall into. The result for the inhabitants who sin in this way is:

"Even the land was defiled so I punished it for its sin". God punished the land! In Jeremiah 23 v 10 we learn that, because of the sin of the people, the land lies parched and the pastures in the desert are withered. Numbers 35 v 34 says "Do not defile the land where you live". In Malachi 4 v 6 the Lord says that in certain circumstances He will strike the land with a curse.

Have you ever thought about the economic situation in Wales? Since the end of the Christian Revival we have seen the mining industry cease production. We are sitting on huge reserves of coal and yet we ship it into Wales from Russia.

My home is on the edge of a huge forestry area. My friend has a sawmill in the centre of that forestry but he is unable to cut down trees around his sawmills and produce square timber for use by the fencing and shed-making producers in the area at such rates that would compete with timber that has been cut and planed and imported from such countries as Latvia and Poland.

The once thriving steel industry has almost disappeared and steel is imported from China, who bought some of our steel-making mills and who supply the United Kingdom today.

Wales is such a hard place for farmers. The price of sheep has been as low as one pound per head in the last six years and has risen to a figure that only just sustains the local hill farmers. The farmer who lives across the valley from me is only scraping a living with a few head of cattle and some sheep.

This land of Wales is beautiful with high mountains and deep valleys; it has peninsulas and beaches that are stunning. However, the potential for tourism has never been reached. Parts of Wales qualified for European aid and grants have been given to encourage industry but have failed to encourage investors in the numbers required.

The land of Wales therefore promises much but produces little. What about its inhabitants? There again are spiritual principles involving the land and, in this case, the inhabitants.

When the Israelites went to explore the land of Canaan, whose inhabitants were pagan worshippers, they returned to Moses with a message that is found in Numbers 13 v32 and that is “The land we explored devours those living in it”.

In Ezekiel 36 the Lord tells Ezekiel to “speak to the mountains of Israel” and in v 13 and 16 we see the accusation that “the mountains devour men”.

Let’s take Wales as an example--again it appears as if the people in this nation are being devoured. We see empty chapels and small struggling churches.

Heart disease in Wales is the highest in Europe and statistics related to drug and alcohol abuse rate amongst those in the inner city areas of England. During my time as a police detective, I recognised that, in the eighties, heroin abuse in small towns such as Holyhead, in proportion to population, was higher than that of Liverpool.

In 1974, the largest drugs operation in the world of its time called Operation "Julie", in which I was involved, was centred in Wales. This involved the manufacture of LSD in Aberystwyth and its worldwide distribution. I also led an investigation into the first illicit ecstasy laboratory outside London, which was in Wrexham.

Tinkersdale, a wood near Hawarden, attracts homosexuals from all over the UK in order to exercise their sexual practices. Magazines connected with such activities advertise this area as a meeting place for homosexuals.

There are spiritual principles which can be applied when purifying the land, the most significant and well known verse being in 2 Chronicles 7v14 "If my people, who are called by my name will humble themselves and pray and seek my face and turn from their wicked ways, then will I hear from heaven and will forgive their sin and heal the land."

The land needs to be healed. To follow this with

other examples, we see that in 2 Chronicles 34, in order to purify the land Josiah destroys idols, restores the temple, re-introduces the Law and the commandments of God and then organises a huge Passover celebration.

In 2 Samuel 21, we see that David tries to make amends with the Gibeonites whom Saul had tried to annihilate. David wanted to put the Gibeonites in a place where they could bless the Lord's inheritance, Israel, thus having the effect of actually blessing the Gibeonite people themselves in accordance with Genesis 12, that those who bless Israel will be blessed. The Gibeonites then asked David for seven of Saul's descendants in order that they could kill them, which they did.

However, they exposed their bodies on a hillside for the full period of the barley harvest. We see in Deuteronomy 21v23 that bodies not buried bring a curse on the land and that appears to have been what happened because, at the end of the season, David gathers the bones of both Saul and his descendants and buries them. Then we see in 2 Sam 21v14 that after David had done this, God answered prayers on behalf of the land.

In 2 Samuel 24v25, after David had repented of sin and acted honourably in the eyes of the Lord, the Lord answered prayer on behalf of the land, then the plague which was upon the people of Israel stopped.

Again, if we take Wales as an example, because of the witchcraft and idolatry which is clearly a major problem and as the situation in Machynlleth proves, we can expect that the land will be punished unless we Christians act, because, as we see in 2 Chronicles 7v14, it is the people God has called who must humble themselves.

Paul tells us in Galatians 5 v20 that witchcraft and idolatry are sin, and then there is an open door in the spiritual realm to rebellion, which would then cause us to oppose God and place us under a curse; therefore we have much to repent of.

We can see the results of promiscuity, dishonesty and lawlessness reported every day in our newspapers and on television. I investigated many cases of child abuse and other deplorable crimes which gave me a clear understanding of the depths to which we have fallen as a society. In all these areas we see the consequences such as increases in HIV and sexually transmitted diseases, divorce, increases in benefit fraud and deaths caused by addictions. We have so much data concerning the overall state of the three Nations together that it is clear that the entire UK is in a continual downward slide into deeper sin.

There are nearly 50,000 people in the UK with HIV. In the last five years sexually transmitted diseases have increased by over 50% and in the last 30 years there have been over 6 million abortions in the UK—all these figures are well documented and are the results of decisions and choices of individuals.

However, I want to present some facts about Wales that can only be attributed to something which is beyond the individual's control and that will help us see deeper underlying problems that cannot simply be attributed to individuals' choices to sin.

To enable a clear picture I will use comparative indicators based in statistics produced for the year 2000. The comparisons are made against England and Scotland and are based on a proportionate 1000 head of population. I accept that I have, to an extent, been selective in my use of the data, but I think you will see my point. I will not present the actual Data for this purpose but their findings.

In 2000 Wales had a population of 2.9 million people in comparison with England's population of 49.5million and Scotland's 5 million.

More people claim social security benefits and have long-term illnesses in Wales than in both England and Scotland.

The percentage of people on hospital waiting lists

over a 12-month period is twice that of England and ten times that of Scotland.

Wales also has more Teenage pregnancies, more births outside marriages and a higher number of lone parents. Male, female and youth unemployment is higher in Wales.

There is a higher youth crime rate and Wales has less Police officers. Disadvantaged land, that is land which cannot be used, is higher in Wales.

GDP is 22% lower than England. 16% lower than Scotland and manufacturing productivity is lower with fewer businesses starting in Wales.

Incomes are lower, more are on Social Security benefits and claiming income support whilst fewer households in Wales have savings accounts.

More people in Wales have no qualifications, fewer 15-year-olds get five good GSCE's and more 15-year-olds have no GCSE's while fewer 18-year-olds get 2 or more A Levels and fewer achieve degrees.

Conclusion

I am a Bible-believing Christian and am writing this book principally for other Bible-believing Christians. If the Bible is our authority and the plumb line for the way we live our lives and all that we do, we must know God's Word on every aspect, including our worship.

Having examined the overall picture of worship, albeit very briefly, a story emerges of humankind in rebellion at every turn, of deception and distortion and a continual turning from God's laws and decrees to suit our own ends–it seems some things never change! Satan comes only to steal, kill and destroy.

It is his motive that is behind all of mankind's rebellion and is still behind all that has been detailed here.

We have looked briefly at witchcraft and pagan practice and have seen that paganism has been around for thousands of years and is practiced today, affecting and involving an entire community, businesses and Church, as in the case of Machynlleth. Children are always the target of the pagan message which is a loud, strong and pervasive call in this heathen society today. We have examined some of the spiritual effects and curses both on man and on the land of being involved, even unwittingly, in witchcraft and idolatry, and looked practically at the situation in Wales today.

I believe we have been sucked into pagan worship unwittingly through lack of knowledge but, having examined the Scriptures regarding God's laws for HIS special days, feasts and celebrations, we are now faced with hard choices which fly in the face and beliefs or understanding of about 99% of the Christian population.

God has made it very clear in the Ten Commandments of Exodus 20 that we should NOT in any way practice in the way that the pagans do. Can the following scripture be any clearer?

"You shall have no other gods before me. You shall not make for yourself an idol in the form of anything in heaven above or on the earth beneath or in the waters below. You shall not bow down to them or worship them" (Ex 20:3-5).

In the book of Deuteronomy God specifically speaks about the practices we have described as follows:

"Let no one be found among you who sacrifices his son or daughter in the fire, who practices divination or sorcery, interprets omens, engages in witchcraft, or casts spells, or who is a medium or spiritist or who consults the dead." - Deut 18:10-11

Other scriptures concerning the pagan world:

"'Do not turn to mediums or seek out spiritists, for you will be defiled by them. I am the LORD your God." - Lev 19:31

"'I will set my face against the person who turns to mediums and spiritists." - Lev 20:6

"Furthermore, Josiah got rid of the mediums and spiritists, the household gods, the idols and all the other detestable things seen in Judah and Jerusalem. This he did to fulfil the requirements of the law written in the book that Hilkiah the priest had discovered in the temple of the LORD." - 2 Kings 23:24

"When men tell you to consult mediums and spiritists, who whisper and mutter, should not a people enquire of their God? Why consult the dead on behalf of the living?" - Isaiah 8:19

What does God say about what we have examined? First of all it is clear that God, through Moses, has given dates and times for feasts that we as Christians can celebrate Jesus in, because He fulfils each one. These festivals are free from pagan influence and are prophetic in nature showing us clearly all that Christ has done for us. God gave us these dates to separate our thanksgiving times from pagan ritual. We should not see these feasts as only Jewish or "Old Testament" customs–God does not change.

We have seen that God gave Israel these set times to worship Him because they had just left a community who were worshipping other gods at set times and they were about to enter a land where the Canaanites were doing the same. God needed to protect them from being aligned to paganism in any way so that they could remain separate and fight their battles without infiltration from the enemy. The same applies to us today –God does not change.

Paul discovered what it was like to come against the idolaters of his day. His gospel message affected the economy. The following scripture speaks to us in these times, particularly concerning such places as Machynlleth where the local economy is supported by occult practice and the making of idols.

"About that time there arose a great disturbance about the Way. A silversmith named Demetrius, who made silver shrines of Artemis, brought in no little business for the craftsmen.

He called them together, along with the workmen in

related trades, and said: "Men, you know we receive a good income from this business. And you see and hear how this fellow Paul has convinced and led astray large numbers of people here in Ephesus and in practically the whole province of Asia. He says that man-made gods are no gods at all. There is danger not only that our trade will lose its good name, but also that the temple of the great goddess Artemis will be discredited, and the goddess herself, who is worshiped throughout the province of Asia and the world, will be robbed of her divine majesty."

When they heard this, they were furious and began shouting: "Great is Artemis of the Ephesians!" Soon the whole city was in an uproar. The people seized Gaius and Aristarchus, Paul's traveling companions from Macedonia, and rushed as one man into the theatre. Paul wanted to appear before the crowd, but the disciples would not let him." Even some of the officials of the province, friends of Paul, sent him a message begging him not to venture into the theatre. The assembly was in confusion: Some were shouting one thing, some another. Most of the people did not even know why they were there." - Acts 19:23-32

Paul in this situation preached correctly from the Torah together with the Good News of the Resurrection of Jesus, the Jewish Messiah. He did not join Demetrius or align himself to the ways of Demetrius but he remained separate, holding fast to God's ways and preaching against the gods of the time.

Paul himself was a member of the first Church, which was called the Synagogue of the Nazarene, led by James the Just, brother of Jesus. This congregation met in the Synagogue as all Jews but they taught Jesus the Messiah, crucified as the sacrificial lamb and had risen from the dead. The only time anyone could join this assembly was at Pentecost when one had to denounce all the works of Satan, and that included pagan traditions, proclaim Jesus as Risen and be baptised. These men who knew Jesus so well would never have joined with the Church as it is today.

As Christians in today's confused society, we have no option but to walk closely with the Lord and His Word. There is simply no room for asking questions of other faiths or new age religions that have already taken their toll on our Faith over the last 2000 years.

A Bishop recently wrote to me suggesting that I read the books by Dr John Drane, entitled "What is the New Age saying to The Church?" and "What is the New Age still saying to The Church?" I cannot understand why he should do this, as John Drane is a doctor in Gnostic studies and has just co-written a book called “Beyond Prediction”, which advises Christians to use the Tarot cards to reach a deeper spiritual experience.

This recommendation is in complete opposition to the Word of God. Where does this kind of Christian understanding fit within the requirements for us to be separate in accordance with the laws of God?

God called the Israelites to be separate from idolatry because, by being connected to it they could not drive out the Canaanites from the land. That is also why He told the Israelites not to marry Canaanite women so that there would be no opportunities to be embroiled in idolatrous worship.

We see that in the book of 2 Kings 18:4 Hezekiah removed all the idols in the land. He also broke into pieces the bronze snake that Moses had made because the Israelites were worshipping it and burning incense to it.

This shows us that, even when an object is made in remembrance of a sacred event, when it is worshipped it becomes an idol. Does this speak of many things today?

If we don’t return to our foundations and the fundamental beliefs given to us through scripture then we can only expect that those who teach and practice witchcraft will continue to do so without the challenge of a strong Church influencing the next generation.

Paul tells us in Romans 11 v 17 that we are grafted into Israel, that we share in Abraham's inheritance. Consequently, we must see that the early Church founders' instructions to move away from all Jewish practices, i.e. the Passover, attempt to lead us away from the truth and strip us of a God-ordained blessing.

Of course, they have been successful, as we still don't worship at the fixed times of the Lord 1700 years after they decreed otherwise.

We are praying for the blessing of God to return to this Nation of Wales that once saw revival but now has returned to its pagan ways. We are praying that those who practice witchcraft will come to repentance and salvation, and we are praying that the Church in this Nation will stand for the truth and give a clear message.

We are called by God to humble ourselves and pray against the pagan practice that is defiling our land but whilst we are worshipping alongside pagans in their ways and on their festivals we are not separated, therefore, we are weakened spiritually and our prayers are not touching Heaven.

We as a congregation have not celebrated the Crucifixion and resurrection at Easter but have done so at the correct time–Passover and we are following the ordained festivals of God with a change to Sabbath worship as the next step. This, I believe, is where the Church needs to be in order to purify the land we live in.

We cannot remain in a place whereby the accuser of the brethren tells us that we are worshipping him at the winter solstice, the birthday of Cernunos, when we should be celebrating the birthday of Jesus during the Feast of Tabernacles.

To be in the strongest spiritual position for the Lord to use us against witchcraft in our Nation we should return to the Feasts of the Lord and ignore the feasts of Satan himself. Neither can we continue to teach our children the ways of the pagan.

This is such a hard challenge to the Christian Church—one that I suspect very few will take up. For me and for my church it has been a process of understanding and revelation which has convinced us that this is the right way forward.

I am well aware that the accusation of "fundamentalist" or suchlike will be thrown at me—I gladly pick these up as I see in my Saviour, Jesus Christ, a radical fundamentalist who was not afraid to say the things that challenged and offended the order and authorities of the day, yet he fulfilled the word and laws of God. I also see in Paul and the apostles a passion and zeal for truth, holiness and righteousness in the midst of wickedness that sadly is missing in our westernised, materialistic, self-satisfied and all-embracing culture.

I would rather be called names and counted amongst their number as I bow before the Lord on judgment day than bow the knee now to other gods.

I have presented my case. I will leave you with the question:

Are we followers of the Craft or followers of Christ?

"You shall have no other gods before Me.

You shall not make for yourself an idol in the form of anything in heaven above or on the earth beneath or in the waters below.

You shall not bow down to them or worship them; for I, the LORD your God, am a jealous God, punishing the children for the sin of the fathers to the third and fourth generation of those who hate Me." - Ex 20:3-5

Reading List

The Holy Bible—New International Version
Popular Cross Reference Edition, Hodder & Stoughton, first published 1979

A History of the Jewish People, H.H. Benson
Harvard University Press Cambridge, Massachusetts 0-674-39731-2

The Historical Jesus, Gerd Theissen & Annette Merz, SCM Press 0-334-02696-2

From Sunday to Sabbath, Samuele Bacchiocchi
The Pontifical Gregorian University Press, Rome
Published 1977

Jesus in the Feasts of Israel, Richard Booker
Destiny Image Publishers, Shippensburg PA
0-914903-98-5

Free from Freemasonry, Ron G. Campbell
Regal Books 0-8307-2383-8

Christian Set Yourself Free From Freemasonry
Derek Robert, Freedom Ministries International
0-9538828-6-1

A Light in the Land, Gwyn Davies
Bryntirion Press, 1-85049-181-X

Heresies Ancient & Modern, J. Oswald Sandders
Marshall, Morgan & Scott, 1948

The Green Man, Jeremy Harte
Pitkin 1-84165-045-5

Honest To Goddess, Geraint ap Iorwerth
Crescent 1-84086-001-4

Raising Witches, Ashleen O'Gaea
New Page Books 1-56414-631-6

Beyond Prediction
John Drane, Ross Clifford & Philip Johnson
Lion Publishing 0-7459-5035-3

Jesus and the Gods of the New Age
Ross Clifford & Philip Johnson
Lion Publishing, 0-7459-5060-4

A Celtic Journey, William Metcalfe
Celtica 0-9544108-0-7

About the Author

Pastor Mike Fryer is a retired National Crime Squad Detective and is now a pastor of Father's House Sabbath Congregation in North Wales and founder of Christian for Zion UK.

Father's House is a congregation which follows The Lords Festivals including Sabbath with passionate Worship and a strong emphasis on the word. Father's House also works alongside the Jewish Community in Israel and the UK to build strong relationships.

Mike graduated in Holocaust Studies in 2009, having studied over a period of 4 years at Yad Vashem. He is a regular visitor to Israel, particularly to the Southern towns, who are regularly bombarded with rockets from Gaza. Mike teaches on the Sabbath, The Lords Feasts, the period of the False Messiah and Christian anti-Semitism including Paganism in the Church.

Mike has written a number of booklets to help us understand the Feasts, Sabbath and some of the issues surrounding our Christian practice. He also wrote a small book on dealing with the occult and Wiccan practice in Wales. In 2000, Mike wrote the Hidden Treasure Course, a seven session course about Israel which he, along with a team of instructors, teach throughout the UK, Ireland, Europe and Russia. The course is repeated regularly on Revelation TV.

Mike's heart is to help the church find its Jewish identity through education and encouragement and to help all in Christendom, understand our past with the aim of preventing the return of the antisemitism/antizionism of old which resulted in the Holocaust amongst other atrocities.

Printed in Great Britain
by Amazon